CHURCH
MEMBER'S
HANDBOOK

CHURCH MEMBER'S HANDBOOK

AN EASY-TO-READ GUIDE TO
THE MANUAL OF THE CHURCH OF THE NAZARENE

Revised Edition (2017-2021)

Neville Bartle • Scott Stargel

PS

Prairie Star Publications

Published by Prairie Star Publications
Lenexa, Kansas (USA)

TABLE OF CONTENTS

NOTE TO THE READER

This small book is a guide to help church members better understand the Church of the Nazarene. It will show you what we Nazarenes believe, how we govern ourselves, and what our purpose is.

The church has an official book called *The Manual of the Church of the Nazarene,* but we usually just call it "the Manual." It is a legal document, and it is very detailed. Many people find it difficult to read and understand, even some who speak English as their first language. So, we prepared this book as an easy-to-read summary of the main points of the Manual, focusing on the parts that relate to the local church and district activities.

While we were very careful in preparing this book, please remember that the Manual is the official source. Throughout the book, you will see a paragraph mark that looks like this: ¶. It is followed by numbers. These numbers refer to sections in the 2017-2021 version of theManual. Look there for additional information. You may view or download a copy of the official Manual at *nazarene.org/manual.*

May God bless you as you follow him!

— *Neville Bartle and Scott Stargel*

OUR MISSION STATEMENT

*The work of the Church of the Nazarene
is to introduce all people to the
transforming grace of God who forgives
our sins and cleanses our hearts
through the blood of Jesus Christ.*

*Our mission is "to make Christlike
disciples in the nations," to bring
believers into congregations (church
membership), and to instruct them so
that they may be involved in ministry.*

*Our goal is to see people living holy lives
through the power of the Holy Spirit
for the glory of God.*

CHAPTER ONE

THE CORE VALUES OF THE CHURCH OF THE NAZARENE

The core values represent our highest priorities and our most deeply held beliefs. They define who we are and what motivates us. We use three words to summarize these values: Christian, holiness, and mission.

Christian

We are a Christian people, united with all true believers in proclaiming Jesus Christ as Lord. We believe that God loves us so much that he gave his only son, Jesus, to be our Saviour. We believe that because of the sacrificial death of Jesus, all people may receive forgiveness of sins and be restored to a right relationship with God.

Since we have been reconciled to God, we believe that we must also be reconciled to one another. We should love each other in the same way that God loved us; we should forgive each other because he forgave us.

We accept the Bible as the source of spiritual truth. We affirm the beliefs and historic creeds of the Christian faith. We treasure our place in what is called the Wesleyan-Holiness tradition. By

"Wesleyan," we connect ourselves to the teachings of John and Charles Wesley who sparked a worldwide spiritual awakening in the 18th Century. By "Holiness," we connect ourselves to the spiritual revivals of the 19th and 20th Century, which were spurred by leaders such as Phineas Bresee, Charles Finney, and Phoebe Palmer with their firmly held belief that God desires to sanctify believers, transforming them into more Christlike disciples.

Holiness

We are a holiness people. The Bible, which we call the Scriptures, and the grace of God call us to worship and love him with our whole heart, soul, mind, and strength, and our neighbours as ourselves.

We believe that, in response to our faith, the Holy Spirit begins to transform and empower us day by day to be a people of love, spiritual discipline, ethical and moral purity, compassion, and justice. It is the work of the Holy Spirit that restores us in the image of God and produces in us the character of Christ. Holiness in the life of believers is most clearly understood as Christlikeness.

Mission

We are a people with a mission to spread the Good News all over the world. Our mission statement is simple: to *make Christlike disciples in the nations.*

Our mission begins as we gather together for worship and then moves outward into the world.

It is expressed as we receive new believers into the fellowship and start new worshiping congregations.

We share God's love for those who are lost and his compassion for the poor and broken by helping to meet the real needs of hurting people. We are committed to inviting people to faith, to caring for those in need and to including in our fellowship all who will call upon the name of the Lord.

We are committed to train and educate our people so that men and women will be equipped as Christian leaders to accomplish the service God calls us to.

CHAPTER TWO

THE ARTICLES OF FAITH

Often, people will ask us, "What do Nazarenes believe?" There is no simple answer to that question, though we might say with Paul, "Jesus is Lord!" While that is a powerful statement, it does not give us very much information.

In order to state precisely our beliefs, Nazarenes followed the tradition of thousands of years of Christian history by adopting an official creed. A creed is a list of statements that usually start with the phrase, "We believe." It summarizes the Church's most important beliefs.

The following is an easy-to-read version of the articles of faith. The official statements are found at the beginning of our constitution in the Manual. They have evolved over time to more accurately reflect changes in language, as well as the Church's understanding of the timeless truths found in the Bible. Each article has several scripture references at the end to show the Biblical basis for it.

Article 1: The Triune God

We believe in one God who is eternal and without limits. He is the creator and the ruler of the universe. He sustains all things. God is holy in every part of his being. He is holy light and holy love. God is one being whose nature is triune. He is revealed to us as Father, Son, and Holy Spirit: the Trinity. [¶1]

Genesis 1; Leviticus 19:2; Deuteronomy 6:4-5; Isaiah 5:16; 6:1-7; 40:18-31; Matthew 3:16-17; 28:19-20; John 14:6-27; 1 Corinthians 8:6; 2 Corinthians 13:14; Galatians 4:4-6; Ephesians 2:13-18; 1 John 1:5; 4:8

Article 2: Jesus Christ

We believe in Jesus Christ, the second person of the Trinity, who has always been one with the Father. He became incarnate by the Holy Spirit and was born of the Virgin Mary. He is not a man who became a god, nor is he a god who simply appeared to be a man. Instead, he is fully God and fully human: two natures combined into one, the God-man.

We believe that Jesus Christ died for our sins. He was resurrected from the dead and took again his body with all things related to the perfection of humanity. He ascended into heaven where he now intercedes for us. [¶2]

Matthew 1:20-25; 16:15-16; Luke 1:26-35; John 1:1-18; Acts 2:22-36; Romans 8:3, 32-34; Galatians 4:4-5; Philippians 2:5-11; Colossians 1:12-22; 1 Timothy 6:14-16; Hebrews 1:1-5; 7:22-28; 9:24-28; 1 John 1:1-3; 4:2-3, 15

Article 3: The Holy Spirit

We believe in the Holy Spirit, the third person of the Trinity, who continually works in the Church of Christ and through it. He convinces the world of sin, and he gives new life to those who repent and believe. He sanctifies believers. The Holy Spirit guides into all truth as revealed in Jesus Christ. [¶3]

John 7:39; 14:15-18, 26; 16:7-15; Acts 2:33; 15:8-9; Romans 8:1-27; Galatians 3:1-14; 4:6; Ephesians 3:14-21; 1 Thessalonians 4:7-8; 2 Thessalonians 2:13; 1 Peter 1:2; 1 John 3:24; 4:13

Article 4: The Holy Scriptures

We believe that the Bible is fully and divinely inspired. The entirety of the sixty-six books of the Old and the New Testaments reveal without error all that we need to know for our salvation. All our articles of faith must be based on this understanding of the Bible. [¶4]

Luke 24:44-47; John 10:35; 1 Corinthians 15:3-4; 2 Timothy 3:15-17; 1 Peter 1:10-12; 2 Peter 1:20-21

Article 5: Sin

We believe that sin came into the world when our first parents, Adam and Eve, disobeyed God. Their sin brought death into creation. We believe that there are two kinds of sin: original sin and personal sin.

We believe that all people are born with a corrupted nature, called original sin or depravity. This nature separates us from original righteousness, which is the pure state of our first parents at the time that God created them. We are spiritually dead and live continually inclined to evil. We believe that original sin remains within the heart of the Christian until it is fully cleansed by the baptism with the Holy Spirit.

Original sin is different from sinning. It is an inherited inclination that drives us to commit sinful acts. People are not judged guilty for original sin until they either neglect or reject God's remedy for it.

Personal sin, also called actual sin, is the act of intentionally breaking a known law by persons who are capable of understanding their actions. Such sins should not be confused with involuntary and inescapable limitations that are the residual results of the Fall. Sins are not the same as mistakes, failures, faults, or other involuntary actions that do not conform to a standard of perfect conduct. However, these limitations are not the same as sins of the spirit. Sins of the spirit include attitudes and actions that are contrary to the Spirit of Christ. Personal sin is primarily and essentially the breaking of the law of love, which may be defined as unbelief in Jesus Christ. [¶5]

Original sin: Genesis 3; 6:5; Job 15:14; Psalm 51:5; Jeremiah 17:9-10; Mark 7:21-23; Romans 1:18-25; 5:12-14; 7:1-8:9; 1 Corinthians 3:1-4; Galatians 5:16-25; 1 John 1:7-8

Personal sin: Matthew 22:36-40 (with 1 John 3:4); John 8:34-36;
16:8-9; Romans 3:23; 6:15-23; 8:18-24; 14:23; 1 John 1:9-2:4;
3:7-10

Article 6: The Atonement

We believe that Jesus Christ suffered, bled, and died on the cross to bring God and human beings into a right relationship. This is called the atonement. It provides the remedy for all human sin, and it is the only basis of salvation. Jesus Christ died for all people. The grace of God provides salvation for children and for those incapable of making decisions for themselves. All others must repent and believe to be saved. [¶6]

Isaiah 53:5-6, 11; Mark 10:45; Luke 24:46-48; John 1:29; 3:14-17; Acts 4:10-12; Romans 3:21-26; 4:17-25; 5:6-21; 1 Corinthians 6:20; 2 Corinthians 5:14-21; Galatians 1:3-4; 3:13-14; Colossians 1:19-23; 1 Timothy 2:3-6; Titus 2:11-14; Hebrews 2:9; 9:11-14; 13:12; 1 Peter 1:18- 21; 2:19-25; 1 John 2:1-2

Article 7: Prevenient grace

We believe that the grace of God, through Jesus Christ, is free and given to all people. It empowers them to choose to turn from sin to righteousness, to believe on Jesus Christ for pardon, and to receive cleansing from sin. The grace of God empowers people to live in ways that are pleasing to God and acceptable to him. This is called "prevenient grace."

We believe that humanity was created in the image of God, which included the ability to choose between good and evil. This is known as moral responsibility. Because of the sin of Adam and Eve, all people are born with a corrupt nature. By their own natural strength, they cannot turn to faith and call upon God, and they cannot do good works to save themselves. [¶7]

Image of God and moral responsibility: Genesis 1:26-27; 2:16-17; Deuteronomy 28:1-2; 30:19; Joshua 24:15; Psalm 8:3-5; Isaiah 1:8-10; Jeremiah 31:29-30; Ezekiel 18:1-4; Micah 6:8; Romans 1:19-20; 2:1-16; 14:7-12; Galatians 6:7-8

Natural inability: Job 14:4; 15:14; Psalms 14:1-4; 51:5; John 3:6a; Romans 3:10-12; 5:12-14, 20a; 7:14-25

Free grace and works of faith: Ezekiel 18:25-26; John 1:12-13; 3:6b; Acts 5:31; Romans 5:6-8, 18; 6:15-16, 23; 10:6-8; 11:22; 1 Corinthians 2:9-14; 10:1-12; 2 Corinthians 5:18-19; Galatians 5:6; Ephesians 2:8-10; Philippians 2:12-13; Colossians 1:21-23; 2 Timothy 4:10a; Titus 2:11-14; Hebrews 2:1-3; 3:12-15; 6:4-6; 10:26-31; James 2:18-22; 2 Peter 1:10-11; 2:20-22

Article 8: Repentance

We believe that the Holy Spirit graciously gives a penitent heart and the hope of mercy to all who will repent. Then, they can believe and receive pardon and spiritual life. Salvation requires repentance, which is a sincere and thorough change of mind about sin. Repentance involves a sense of personal guilt and voluntarily turning away from sin. It is required because we all, through our actions or our intentions, became sinners against God.

We believe that it is possible for someone to return to sin and reject the faith. Those who return to sin will be hopelessly and eternally lost unless they repent of their sins. However, we believe that those who are born again do not need to return to sin. Instead, they may continue to live, without interruption, in fellowship with God because of the power of the Holy Spirit who lives in them. The Holy Spirit witnesses to our spirits that we are children of God. [¶8]

2 Chronicles 7:14; Psalms 32:5-6; 51:1-17; Isaiah 55:6-7; Jeremiah 3:12-14; Ezekiel 18:30-32; 33:14-16; Mark 1:14-15; Luke 3:1-14; 13:1-5; 18:9-14; Acts 2:38; 3:19; 5:31; 17:30-31; 26:16-18; Romans 2:4; 2 Corinthians 7:8-11; 1 Thessalonians 1:9; 2 Peter 3:9

Article 9: Salvation

Justification. We believe that all who believe in Jesus Christ and receive him as Lord and Savior are justified. This means that God fully and freely pardons their guilt and releases them from the penalty of their sins. He accepts them as righteous.

Regeneration. We believe that God freely regenerates all those who repent and believe in Jesus Christ as Lord and Savior. He provides them with a new spiritual life and a new moral nature, which is capable of faith, love, and obedience to God. This is called the new birth.

Adoption. We believe that God, who freely justifies and regenerates new believers, adopts them as children into the family of God.

Justification, regeneration, and adoption happen at the same moment upon a person's repentance and faith in Christ. The Holy Spirit witnesses to us that God has accomplished these acts of grace. [¶9]

Luke 18:14; John 1:12-13; 3:3-8; 5:24; Acts 13:39; Romans 1:17; 3:21-26, 28; 4:5-9, 17-25; 5:1, 16-19; 6:4; 7:6; 8:1, 15-17; 1 Corinthians 1:30; 6:11; 2 Corinthians 5:17-21; Galatians 2:16-21; 3:1-14, 26; 4:4-7; Ephesians 1:6-7; 2:1, 4-5; Philippians 3:3-9; Colossians 2:13; Titus 3:4-7; 1 Peter 1:23; 1 John 1:9; 3:1-2, 9; 4:7; 5:1, 9-13, 18

Article 10: Holiness

Sanctification. We believe that sanctification is the work of God that transforms believers into the likeness of Jesus Christ. This work is accomplished by God's grace through the Holy Spirit. Sanctification starts with regeneration, which happens at the same time as justification. It is also called initial sanctification. It continues through entire sanctification and the continuous work of the Holy Spirit as he perfects believers, transforming them into Christlikeness. It results in glorification, at which time they are fully conformed to the image of the Son.

Entire sanctification. We believe that after regeneration there is an additional work of God by which believers are freed from original sin, which is also called depravity. Believers enter into a state of entire devotion to God and holy obedience that is perfected love.

Entire sanctification is the result of the baptism with the Holy Spirit, which is also called the infilling of the Holy Spirit. It includes the cleansing of the heart from sin and the abiding presence of the Holy Spirit. He empowers the believer to live and to serve like Jesus Christ.

Entire sanctification is possible because of Jesus's sacrifice. It happens instantaneously by grace through faith. It is preceded by the total commitment of a believer to God, which is called entire consecration. The Holy Spirit witnesses to us that he has accomplished this.

This experience is known by various terms that represent its different phases: "Christian perfection," "perfect love," "heart unity," "the baptism with the Holy Spirit," "the infilling of the Holy Spirit," "the fullness of the blessing," and "Christian holiness."

We believe there is clear distinction between a pure heart and a mature character. A pure heart happens in an instant as a result of entire sanctification. A mature character happens over time through the process of growing in grace.

We believe that the person who is entirely sanctified has a godly desire to grow in grace as a Christlike disciple. This growth is not automatic. It must be consciously nurtured through spiritual development and improvement in order to develop a Christlike character and personality. Those who do not intentionally work at spiritual growth will damage their witness, and they may frustrate God's grace and eventually lose it.

By participating in the means of grace, believers grow in grace and in wholehearted love of God and neighbor. These means of grace include especially fellowship, the spiritual disciplines, and the sacraments of the Church. [¶10]

Jeremiah 31:31-34; Ezekiel 36:25-27; Malachi 3:2-3; Matthew 3:11-12; Luke 3:16-17; John 7:37-39; 14:15-23; 17:6-20; Acts 1:5; 2:1-4; 15:8-9; Romans 6:11-13, 19; 8:1-4, 8-14; 12:1-2; 2 Corinthians 6:14-7:1; Galatians 2:20; 5:16-25; Ephesians 3:14-21; 5:17-18, 25-27; Philippians 3:10-15; Colossians 3:1-17; 1 Thessalonians 5:23-24; Hebrews 4:9-11; 10:10-17; 12:1-2; 13:12; 1 John 1:7, 9

"Christian perfection," "perfect love": Deuteronomy 30:6; Matthew 5:43-48; 22:37-40; Romans 12:9-21; 13:8-10; 1 Corinthians 13; Philippians 3:10-15; Hebrews 6:1; 1 John 4:17-18

"Heart purity": Matthew 5:8; Acts 15:8-9; 1 Peter 1:22; 1 John 3:3

"Baptism with the Holy Spirit": Jeremiah 31:31-34; Ezekiel 36:25-27; Malachi 3:2-3; Matthew 3:11-12; Luke 3:16-17; Acts 1:5; 2:1-4; 15:8-9

"Fullness of the blessing": Romans 15:29

"Christian holiness": Matthew 5:1-7:29; John 15:1-11; Romans 12:1-15:3; 2 Corinthians 7:1; Ephesians 4:17-5:20; Philippians 1:9-11; 3:12-15; Colossians 2:20-3:17; 1 Thessalonians 3:13; 4:7-8; 5:23; 2 Timothy 2:19-22; Hebrews 10:19-25; 12:14; 13:20-21; 1 Peter 1:15-16; 2 Peter 1:1-11; 3:18; Jude 20-21

Article 11: The Church

We believe in the Church, which is the community that confesses Jesus Christ as Lord. It is the people of God's covenant who are made new in

Christ. The Church is the Body of Christ called together by the Holy Spirit through the Word.

God calls the Church to be a visible expression of the unity and the fellowship of the Spirit. The Church demonstrates this unity as it obeys Christ and lives holy lives. Believers are mutually accountable to one another. This unity is visible in worship through the preaching of the Word, by participating in the sacraments, and by ministry in the name of Jesus Christ.

The mission of the Church is to share the work of Christ as he redeems and reconciles the world in the power of the Spirit. The Church fulfills its mission by making disciples. We do this through evangelizing, educating, showing compassion, working for justice, and proclaiming the kingdom of God. [¶11]

Exodus 19:3; Jeremiah 31:33; Matthew 8:11; 10:7; 16:13-19, 24; 18:15-20; 28:19-20; John 17:14-26; 20:21-23; Acts 1:7-8; 2:32-47; 6:1-2; 13:1; 14:23; Romans 2:28-29; 4:16; 10:9-15; 11:13-32; 12:1-8; 15:1-3; 1 Corinthians 3:5-9; 7:17; 11:1, 17-33; 12:3, 12-31; 14:26-40; 2 Corinthians 5:11-6:1; Galatians 5:6, 13-14; 6:1-5, 15; Ephesians 4:1-17; 5:25-27; Philippians 2:1-16; 1 Thessalonians 4:1-12; 1 Timothy 4:13; Hebrews 10:19-25; 1 Peter 1:1-2, 13; 2:4-12, 21; 4:1-2, 10-11; 1 John 4:17; Jude 24; Revelation 5:9-10

Article 12: Baptism

We believe that Christian baptism is a sacrament commanded by our Lord. It signifies that a person has accepted the benefits of the atonement and has become a part of the Body of Christ. It is a means of grace that proclaims the believer's faith in Jesus Christ as Savior. Baptism demonstrates a believer's desire to follow Jesus Christ in obedience, holiness, and righteousness.

Young children and the morally innocent are participants in the new covenant. Therefore, they may be baptized at the request of their parents or guardians. The church pledges to provide Christian training. A person may be baptized by sprinkling, pouring, or immersion. [¶12]

Matthew 3:1-7; 28:16-20; Acts 2:37-41; 8:35-39; 10:44-48; 16:29-34; 19:1- 6; Romans 6:3-4; Galatians 3:26-28; Colossians 2:12; 1 Peter 3:18-22

Article 13: The Lord's Supper

We believe that the Lord's Supper is a sacrament that Jesus Christ established. It proclaims his life, suffering, sacrificial death, resurrection, and the hope of his coming again. It is a means of grace in which Christ is present by the Spirit. All are invited to participate by faith in Christ and to be renewed in life, in salvation, and in unity as the Church. All should come respectfully, appreciating its significance. By participating in this sacrament, we testify to the Lord's death until he comes again. Those who have faith in Christ and who love the people of God are invited to participate as often as possible. [¶13]

Exodus 12:1-14; Matthew 26:26-29; Mark 14:22-25; Luke 22:17-20; John 6:28-58; 1 Corinthians 10:14-21; 11:23-32

Article 14: Divine healing

We believe in the biblical doctrine of divine healing. We encourage our people to pray in faith for the healing of the sick. We also believe that God heals through the means of medical science. [¶14]

2 Kings 5:1-19; Psalm 103:1-5; Matthew 4:23-24; 9:18-35; John 4:46-54; Acts 5:12-16; 9:32-42; 14:8-15; 1 Corinthians 12:4-11; 2 Corinthians 12:7-10; James 5:13-16

Article 15:
The Second Coming of Christ

We believe that the Lord Jesus Christ will come to earth again. Those believers who died will be resurrected and rise to be with him. We who are alive and abiding in Jesus Christ will be carried away with the risen ones to meet the Lord in the air. From then on, we will always be with the Lord. [¶15]

Matthew 25:31-46; John 14:1-3; Acts 1:9-11; Philippians 3:20-21; 1 Thessalonians 4:13-18; Titus 2:11-14; Hebrews 9:26-28; 2 Peter 3:3-15; Revelation 1:7-8; 22:7-20

Article 16:
Resurrection, judgment, and destiny

We believe in the resurrection of the dead. That is to say, the bodies of both the just and the unjust will be raised to life and united with their spirits. "Those who have done what is good will rise to live, and those who have done what is evil will rise to be condemned."

We believe in a future judgement in which every person will appear before God to be judged according to his or her deeds in this life.

Those who refuse to repent will suffer eternally in hell. We believe that those who are saved by faith in Jesus Christ and who obediently follow him are assured of a glorious and everlasting life. [¶16]

Genesis 18:25; 1 Samuel 2:10; Psalm 50:6; Isaiah 26:19; Daniel 12:2-3; Matthew 25:31-46; Mark 9:43-48; Luke 16:19-31; 20:27-38; John 3:16-18; 5:25-29; 11:21-27; Acts 17:30-31; Romans 2:1-16; 14:7-12; 1 Corinthians 15:12-58; 2 Corinthians 5:10; 2 Thessalonians 1:5-10; Revelation 20:11-15; 22:1-15

DO YOU KNOW ALL OF THE ARTICLES OF FAITH?

Memorizing the articles of faith will help you answer the question "What do Nazarenes believe?" To help you memorize them, visit *www.studymaps.org* for a visual guide.

CHAPTER THREE

MEMBERSHIP
IN THE CHURCH OF THE NAZARENE

What does the word "church" mean?

The Bible says that there is a Book of Life where the names of all believers are written down (Revelation 20:12). Nazarenes do not believe that we are the only ones whose names are written in that book. Instead, we believe that all believers, including those who have already died, are part of the Body of Christ, which is the Church. We state this clearly in our eleventh article of faith [¶11].

However, a word often has more than one meaning, and this is very true of the word "church." Believers gather together in different places all over the world to worship, fellowship, and minister to those in their community. Sometimes these are called congregations or assemblies, but we normally call them "local churches." Sometimes they meet in a fancy building that is also called "a church." Other churches may meet under a shady tree or in a rented storefront. No matter where the local church gathers, God is there, present and active [¶18].

Yet another use of the word "church" is when we talk about a denomination. So, while there are individual Churches of the Nazarene all over the world, there is also a global organization called the Church of the Nazarene. It is a collection of all those people who voluntarily associate themselves with it and call themselves Nazarenes.

This global organization, sometimes called the International Church of the Nazarene, has a set of core values and priorities, which we discussed in chapter one [¶19].

The statement of belief

While the articles of faith of the Church of the Nazarene give specific details about all our important doctrines, we realize that not everyone will understand those statements. Therefore, the Manual contains a shorter declaration called the "statement of belief" [¶20]. The pastor will ask each person who wants to become a member to affirm this statement before joining the Church of the Nazarene. Here is what it says:

We believe ...

...in one God—the Father, Son, and Holy Spirit.

...that the Old and New Testament Scriptures, given by plenary inspiration,[1] contain all truth necessary to faith and Christian living.

---

1 "Plenary inspiration" means that God was involved in the entire process of creating the Bible.

DO YOU HAVE TROUBLE WITH THE STATEMENT OF BELIEF?

If you do not understand any part of the statement of belief, or if you do not agree with some of it, talk to the pastor. There is no hurry to become a member, and we do not want anyone to feel forced to join. However, we encourage people to continue to worship and to serve in a Nazarene church, if they are regularly attending, even though they may not become members.

...that human beings are born with a fallen nature, and are, therefore, inclined to evil, and that continually.

...that the finally impenitent are hopelessly and eternally lost.

...that the atonement through Jesus Christ is for the whole human race; and that whoever repents and believes on the Lord Jesus Christ is justified, regenerated, and saved from the dominion of sin.

...that believers are to be sanctified wholly, subsequent to regeneration, through faith in the Lord Jesus Christ.

...that the Holy Spirit bears witness to the new birth, and also to the entire sanctification of believers.

*...that our Lord will return, the dead will be raised,
and the final judgment will take place.*

The Covenant of Christian Character

Most organizations have rules that their members follow. This is true of the Church of the Nazarene as well. We have two covenants, which are written promises that indicate how we expect our members to live.

People who have accepted Jesus as their Saviour and who desire to join in the fellowship of the Church of the Nazarene should live a godly life. We have the privilege and the duty to seek to be like Christ. The word of God instructs us on how we should live, and the Covenant of Christian Character summarizes these instructions [¶21].

Church members should...

*...love God with all their heart, mind, soul and
strength, and their neighbour as themselves.
(Exodus 20:3-6; Leviticus 19:17-18; Deuteronomy
5:7-10; 6:4-5; Mark 12:28-31; Romans 13:8-10)*

*...share the gospel with those who are not saved,
invite them to church, and seek to lead them to
Christ. (Mathew 28:19-20; Acts 1:8; Romans 1:14-
16; 2 Corinthians 5:18-20)*

*...be courteous to all people. (Ephesians 4:32; Titus
3:2; 1 Peter 2:17; 1 John 3:18)*

...be helpful, kind, patient, and forgiving to fellow Christians. (Romans 12:13; Galatians 6:2, 10; Colossians 3:12-14)

...seek to do good to all who are hungry, sick, imprisoned, and in need. (Matthew 25:35-36; 2 Corinthians 9:8-10; Galatians 2:10; James 2:15-16; 1 John 3:17-18)

...give tithes and offerings to support the work of the church. (Malachi 3:10; Luke 6:38; 1 Corinthians 9:14; 16:2; 2 Corinthians 9:6-10; Philippians 4:15-19)

...attend faithfully the regular church worship services, take communion, and have private and family devotions. (Hebrews 10:25, Acts 2:42; 1 Corinthians 11:23-30; Acts 17:11; 2 Timothy 2:15; 3:14-16; Deuteronomy 6:6-7; Matthew 6:6)

Church members should avoid...

...taking the name of God in vain. (Exodus 20:7; Leviticus 19:12; James 5:12)

...doing unnecessary secular activities on the Lord's Day so that it loses its sacredness. (Exodus 20:8-11; Isaiah 58:13-14; Mark 2:27-28; Acts 20:7; Revelation 1:10)

...all forms of sexual immorality. (Exodus 20:14; Matthew 5:27-32; 1 Corinthians 6:9-11; Galatians 5:19; 1 Thessalonians 4:3-7)

...habits or practices that are destructive to us physically or mentally. We should remember that we are the temples of the Holy Spirit. (Proverbs

20:1; 23:1-3; 1 Corinthians 6:17-20; 2 Corinthians 7:1; Ephesians 5:18).

...quarrelling, gossiping, and spreading stories that hurt the good names of others. (2 Corinthians 12:20; Galatians 5:15; Ephesians 4:30-32; James 3:5-18; 1 Peter 3:9-10)

...dishonesty, cheating in business, and telling lies. (Leviticus 19:10-11; Romans 12:17; 1 Corinthians 6:7-10).

...being proud in dress and behaviour. People should dress in simplicity and modesty so as to reflect a holy life. (Proverbs 29:23; 1 Timothy 2:8-10; James 4:6; 1 Peter 3:3-4; 1 John 2:15-17)

...music, literature, and entertainments that dishonour God. (1 Corinthians 10:31; 2 Corinthians 6:14-17; James 4:4).

We should always...

...be in wholehearted fellowship with the church.

...respect the church leadership.

...remain committed to the Church's doctrines and rules.

...be actively involved in outreach and ministry. (Ephesians 2:18-22; 4:1-3, 11-16; Philippians 2:1-8; 1 Peter 2:9-10)

The Covenant of Christian Conduct

Our first covenant gave a general description of a believer who is striving to be a Christlike disciple. The second covenant speaks more directly to certain activities and issues that influence our walk with God. Below is a shortened version of the Covenant of Christian Conduct that is found in the Manual [¶28-35].

The Christian life

The church joyfully proclaims the good news that we may be delivered from all sin to a new life in Christ. By the grace of God, we Christians should no longer follow the sinful nature and the old patterns of conduct. Instead we are to "put on the new self"—a new and holy way of life and of thinking (Ephesians 4:17-24).

The Church of the Nazarene seeks to relate timeless principles of the Bible to our society in such a way that the doctrines and rules of the church are known and understood in a variety of cultures. We believe that the Ten Commandments provide our basic Christian ethic and should be obeyed.

The International Church of the Nazarene wants to help all its members to develop a holy way of life. The Holy Spirit will help us do this. Members should carefully follow the Covenant of Christian Conduct as a guide to holy living. People who do not follow these guidelines hurt the witness of the church and weaken their own spiritual lives.

Education is very important for the social and spiritual well-being of society. Public schools usually provide only a secular education. Therefore, it is important that the church teach biblical principles and high ethical standards. We do this through Sunday schools, day schools, primary and secondary schools, universities and seminaries. We should teach holiness in our homes. Christians should be encouraged to work in public schools and to provide a Christian witness and influence there.

Church leaders should teach biblical truths that will help people be able to tell the difference between good and evil. It is impossible, and not helpful, to list every known sin in the world. Therefore, it is important that all church members seek the help of the Holy Spirit to distinguish right from wrong. "Test everything. Hold on to the good. Avoid every kind of evil" (1 Thessalonians 5:21-22). However, we have discovered that there are many activities and practices that are harmful to our Christian witness and that weaken us spiritually.

So then, Nazarenes should avoid the following.

Entertainments that destroy Christian values. Christians should follow three important principles as they decide what to do for entertainment. [¶29.1]

1. Christian stewardship applies to relaxation as well as work.

2. Christians are called to live holy lives. There are many books, radio, and television pro-

grams as well as images and videos from the internet that come into our homes. We must avoid any of them that would lead us away from God and holy living. We should support and encourage those programs, books, and websites that are good and helpful.

3. As Christians, we should speak out against entertainments that ignore God or promote evil, violence, and immorality. We should avoid all entertainments that make sin look appealing and exciting, or that undermine God's standard of holiness of heart and life.

We teach our people to use prayerful discernment and to make wise choices that lead to holy living. We should listen to the advice that John Wesley's mother gave him, "Whatever weakens your reason, impairs the tenderness of your conscience, dulls your sense of God, or diminishes your desire for spiritual things, whatever increases the authority of your body over mind, that thing for you is sin."

(Romans 14:7-13; 1 Corinthians 10:31-33; Ephesians 5:1-18; Philippians 4:8-9; 1 Peter 1:13-17; 2 Peter 1:3-11)

Gambling. We should avoid lotteries and other forms of gambling for they destroy both individuals and society. [¶29.2]

(Matthew 6:24-34; 2 Thessalonians 3:6-13; 1 Timothy 6:6-11; Hebrews 13:5-6; 1 John 2:15-17)

Secret organizations. We should not become members of organisations that require people to take an oath of secrecy. [¶29.3]

(1 Corinthians 1:26-31; 2 Corinthians 6:14-7:1; Ephesians 5:11-16; James 4:4; 1 John 2:15-17)

Dancing. We avoid all forms of dancing that hinder our spiritual growth or break down our self-control. [¶29.4]

(Matthew 22:36-39; Romans 12:1-2; 1 Corinthians 10:31-33; Philippians 1:9-11; Colossians 3:1-17)

Drugs. We avoid drinking intoxicating liquor, using tobacco, and using drugs. We also avoid selling such things. The Bible and human experience both show that drinking alcohol, using tobacco, and taking drugs create many social problems. Since our goal is to live a holy life, we should not use these things. The Bible teaches that our body is the temple of the Holy Spirit. Therefore we call our people to total abstinence from all intoxicants. Our lives should always be a good witness to others. [¶29.5]

(Proverbs 20:1; 23:29-24:2; Hosea 4:10-11; Habakkuk 2:5; Romans 13:8; 14:15-21; 15:1-2; 1 Corinthians 3:16-17; 6:9-12, 19-20; 10:31-33; Galatians 5:13-14,21; Ephesians 5:18)

We should not use any drugs, even if they are legal, that affect our thinking or feelings (such as hallucinogenic, stimulants, and depressants). Prescription drugs should only be used under the care of a medical professional. [¶29.6]

(Matthew 22:37-39; 27:34; Romans 12:1-2; 1 Corinthians 6:19-20; 9:24-27)

Marriage and divorce

There are many forces working in society to weaken and destroy marriage and the Christian family. It is important that pastors preach clearly the biblical plan that marriage is to be permanent. Churches need to develop programs that will strengthen and help Christian families.

God designed marriage, and it is the mutual union of one man and one woman for fellowship, helpfulness, and bearing children. People should not enter into marriage hastily but after prayer for God's guidance. The marriage covenant is binding as long as both shall live, and breaking the marriage is a breach of God's plan of the permanence of marriage.

(Genesis 1:26-28, 31; 2:21-24; Malachi 2:13-16; Matthew 19:3-9; John 2:1-11; Ephesians 5:21-6:4; 1 Thessalonians 4:3-8; Hebrews 13:4)

We recognize that some people are forced to divorce against their will, and some people get divorced for legal or physical protection. Divorce is not beyond the forgiving grace of God when this is sought with repentance, faith, and humility.

(Genesis 2:21-24; Mark 10:2-12; Luke 7:36-50; 16:18; John 7:53-8:11; 1 Corinthians 6:9-11; 7:10-16; Ephesians 5:25-33)

Ministers of the Church of the Nazarene should teach their congregations the sacredness of marriage. They should always provide counselling to a couple before conducting any wedding. This also applies to those who have been divorced and wish to remarry. Ministers shall only conduct weddings for those who have a biblical basis for marriage.

Members who are in unhappy marriages should try to find ways to correct the problems. They should do this in harmony with their vows and the clear teachings of Scripture. They should seek to protect the family and not bring shame on Christ or his church. Couples with serious marriage problems should seek counsel and advice from their pastor and other spiritual leaders.

Because of ignorance, sin, and human weakness many people do not follow God's plan. We believe God can help these people just as Jesus helped the woman of Samaria. Where people have divorced and remarried, they are to seek God's grace and his help in their marriage relationship. These people may be accepted as Church members provided they show that they have repented and are aware of the sanctity of marriage. [¶31]

Sexuality

Human sexuality is one expression of the holiness and beauty that God intended for his creation. It is one of the ways in which the covenant between husband and wife is sealed and expressed. Human sexuality is sanctified by God only when it occurs within marriage and expresses love and loyalty.

We should teach our children the sacred character of human sexuality within the context of love, patience, and trust in the Christian home.

Ministers and teachers in the church should state clearly the Christian understanding of human sexuality. They should urge Christians to see it as good and holy, and guard against those things that would weaken and distort it.

All forms of sexual intimacy that occur outside of marriage between a man and a woman are contrary to God's laws.

Homosexuality is one form by which human sexuality is used wrongly. The Church of the Nazarene affirms the biblical position that such acts are sinful. We believe the grace of God is sufficient to overcome the practice of homosexuality, and that the Church must be a welcoming, forgiving, and loving community where hospitality, encouragement, transformation, and accountability are available to all.

(1 Corinthians 6:9-11; Genesis 1:27; 19:1-25; Leviticus 20:13; Romans 1:26-27; 1 Corinthians 6:9-11; 1 Timothy 1:8-10)

[¶31]

The sacredness of human life

The Church of the Nazarene believes that life, even that of an unborn child, is sacred and is given to us by God. We are opposed to abortion. We realize that there are rare cases where the life of the mother, the unborn child, or both are in danger. In such situations, termination of the pregnancy should only be done after sound medical advice and Christian counselling.

Since we are opposed to abortion, we must also be committed to programs that help mothers and children. Where there is an unwanted pregnancy, the church must provide loving support, prayer, and counsel. This may include homes for expectant mothers or the creation of Christian adoption services.

Often people seek abortion because they did not follow Christian standards of sexual responsibility. The church needs to provide clear teaching on human sexuality from a Christian perspective. [¶30]

(Exodus 20:13; 21:12-16; Job 31:15; Psalms 22:9; 139:3-16; Isaiah 44:2, 24; 49:5; Luke 1:23-25, 36-45; Romans 12:1-2; 1 Corinthians 6:16; 7:1; 1 Thessalonians 4:3-6)

Christian stewardship

The Scriptures teach that God is the owner of all persons and all things. We are stewards, or caretakers, of God's creation. We are to care for and use wisely the resources that we have. This includes both our lives and the things we possess. One day we must give an account of our stewardship to God. [¶32]

Tithing. God established a system of giving called "tithing," which means giving one-tenth of our income back to him. This demonstrates both God's ownership and our stewardship. We sometimes call it "storehouse tithing." This phrase is from Malachi 3:10. It means that church members should give their tithe to the one place, the local church. We also give other offerings, in addition to the tithe, to support the whole church at local, district, regional, and general levels. [¶32.1]

Local church obligations. Just as church members give money to the local church, the local church also supports other ministries. We urge our local churches to pay their district, regional, and general obligations on a monthly basis. [¶32.2]

Support of the ministers. "The Lord has commanded that those who preach the gospel should receive their living from the gospel" (1 Corinthians 9:14). Church members give their tithe regularly. From those funds, the church should support its ministers—those whom God has called and give themselves wholly to the work of the ministry. Church boards should pay their pastor every week. [¶32.3]

Life gifts and giving after we die. Christians should be faithful in paying their tithes and giving offerings while they are alive. They should also think of what they will do with the money and possessions that remain when they die. Christians should prayerfully make a legal will and consider giving towards the ongoing work of the church. [¶32.4]

(Malachi 3:8-10; Matthew 6:24-34; 25:31-46; Mark 10:17-31; Luke 12:13-24; 19:11-27; John 15:1-17; Romans 12:1-13; 1 Corinthians 9:7-14; 2 Corinthians 8:1-15; 9:6-15; 1 Timothy 6:6-19; Hebrews 7:8; James 1:27; 1 John 3:16-18)

Church leaders

In the Church of the Nazarene, the pastor and the local leaders share the burden of ministry. These leaders are elected to various positions in the church. Usually, the church members elect them. We urge our people to elect only those members who profess the experience of entire sanctification and who demonstrate a holy life through the grace of God. They should be in harmony with the doctrines, policy, and practices of the Church of the Nazarene. They should be active in the church. This includes supporting the church faithfully in attendance and with tithes and offerings.

Becoming a member
of the Church of the Nazarene

Not everyone who attends our worship services or supports our ministries is a member of the Church of the Nazarene. That is not a problem, since joining the church is voluntary. A church member is a person who has made a public commitment to be actively involved and supportive of the local church [¶107–109.5].

Usually, someone who wants to become a member must attend classes to learn about the Church of the Nazarene: its doctrines, history, rules, government, policies, mission, core values, and priorities. Before a pastor accepts new members into the church, he or she will explain to them the Articles of Faith, the requirements of the Covenant of Christian Character and the Covenant of Christian Conduct, and the purpose and mission of the Church of the Nazarene.

For those who want to join the church, there are four requirements.

A *church member must...*

...***be a Christian.*** *People who want to become members must be saved. When they join the church, the pastor will ask them to affirm that they have accepted Jesus Christ as their Saviour.*

...***agree with the doctrines of the church.*** *In front of the congregation, the pastor will ask those who want to join the Church to affirm the statement of belief of the Church of the Nazarene.*

...***accept the government of the church***. *The requirements are found in the government sections of the manual, the Covenant of Christian Character, and the Covenant of Christian Conduct.*

...***support the church.*** *Members agree to give their time, talent, and treasure to the Church. They agree to attend faithfully the services, to participate in its programs, and to support it financially.*

ARE YOU READY TO BECOME A MEMBER OF THE CHURCH?

If you meet all four of the requirements to become a member, you should talk to the pastor about membership. The pastor will interview you and make a recommendation to a special committee of the church. If the committee approves, the pastor will welcome you as a new member at a public ceremony during a church service.

CHAPTER FOUR

CHURCH ORGANIZATION

There are many different churches and denominations in the world. However, almost all are organized according to one of the three ways:

1. Some churches give their ministers most of the authority.
2. Some churches give the congregation most of the authority.
3. Some churches share the authority between ministers and the congregation.

Phineas Bresee was a minister in the Methodist Church who lived in the western part of the United States. The Methodists had leaders called bishops. Bishops had lots of authority over pastors and churches. Later in his life, Bresee left the Methodists and started many new churches. He felt they needed strong leaders who could encourage and supervise pastors, like bishops. He chose to call them superintendents.

On the eastern side of the United States, there were some churches that, like Bresee, believed that holy living was a biblical truth that the church should preach. However, this group felt that bishops sometimes interfered too much in the affairs of the local church. So, they gave each congregation a lot of authority.

When these two groups decided to come together to form the Church of the Nazarene, they worked hard to find a way to combine these different ideas about church leadership. They agreed that they needed superintendents to counsel and help guide the churches. They also agreed that local churches should have the authority to choose their own pastor and look after their own affairs.

The Church of the Nazarene chose a representative form of government. This means that leaders at all levels of church government are elected. The pastor and the church board share the responsibility of leading and managing the work of the church. However, we believe that churches should not be independent of each other. They should work together. Therefore, the Church of the Nazarene has leaders, still called superintendents, who assist the local churches in fulfilling its mission and objectives. A superintendent is like a team leader or coach who encourages and supports all the pastors in his or her area of responsibility, called a district.

The authority of the superintendents is limited, though, and they should not interfere with the independent action of an organized church. Each church should enjoy the right to select its own pastor, manage its own finances, and handle all the other matters related to its local life and work [¶22-22.3].

There are three levels of church government in the Church of the Nazarene.

1. The Local Church
2. The District Assembly
3. The General Assembly

At each level, we see this collaboration between individual leaders and boards. At the local church, the pastor and the church board work together. Local churches are grouped together into districts, which are led by a district superintendent who works with an advisory board. Together they help guide the churches on the district. The districts are led by six general superintendents who work with the General Board to lead and direct the global church.

To help with administrative tasks, the General Board divides the world into six regions. Each region has a regional director (not superintendent) who helps the general superintendents do their work.

CHAPTER FIVE

THE LOCAL CHURCH

The most important organization in the Church of the Nazarene is the local church.

A dynamic local church is easy to identify. The community knows it as a place where...

...people come together to worship, to learn from God's word, and to hear good preaching.

...people become Christians and grow spiritually.

...people become active church members and share in the church's ministry to others.

A local church is not a building. Instead, it is a group of Christians who became members and agree to support the ministry of the church in their community. It is part of a global denomination called the Church of the Nazarene.

In chapter four, we discussed how a person joins the Church of the Nazarene as a member. Being a member has many privileges, including the important responsibility of participating in official church meetings.

The annual church meeting

A church meeting is a gathering where the members meet together to discuss issues and to make decisions concerning the life, growth, and organization of the local church. Churches have one official church meeting each year, but from time to time, they may call special meetings if an important issue arises [¶113-113.15]. Here are some important details about the meeting.

- The annual church meeting has two main functions: to hear reports and to conduct elections.
- The pastor is the chair of the meeting, the president.
- The secretary of the church board is the secretary of the church meeting.
- The annual church meeting must take place less than three months before the district assembly (see the next chapter for more about district assemblies).
- A member must be at least 15 years old to vote in elections at the meeting.

The annual reports

Each year, everyone hears from the leaders of the different ministries of the church. This is important, so that all the members know what is happening in the church. The pastor will help the leaders prepare. Here is a list of the reports.

- The pastor [¶516.7]
- The secretary of church board [¶135.2]
- The treasurer [¶136.5]
- The Sunday School superintendent [¶146.6]
- The NYI president [¶810.105]

- The NMI president [¶152.2]
- Those with a local preacher's license [¶531.1]
- The presidents or leaders of other groups in the church, such as the Women's Fellowship and the Men's Fellowship.

Elections

Earlier, we discussed the characteristics and requirements of being a leader in the Church of the Nazarene. Based on that description, at the annual church meeting, the church members elect people to the following positions of leadership.

- at least three stewards [¶137]
- at least three trustees [¶141]
- a superintendent of the Sunday School [¶146]
- Sunday School board [¶145]
- Presidents or leaders of other groups, such as the women's ministry president and the men's ministry president
- Delegates to the district assembly, if the church board doesn't elect them [¶22.3; 113.10; 201.1-201.2]

The work of the pastor

A pastor is a minister who has oversight of a local church [¶514]. He or she is either an elder or a licensed minister (someone who received a minister's license from the district assembly) [¶115]. A pastor feels a divine call to preach the Word of

God and to care for God's people. He or she has many responsibilities and the job requires a lot of work. Here is a list of the type of work, divided into two main categories [¶514-522].

The core duties of the pastor are...

...to pray.

...to preach the Word of God.

...to train the people of the church to do ministry (evangelism).

...to perform religious duties (baptism, communion, weddings, and funerals).

...to look after the people of the church, this includes
  - visiting them;
  - caring for the sick and poor;
  - comforting those who mourn;
  - encouraging people to become Christlike disciples;
  - helping sinners to repent and to turn to God;
  - helping Christians to be filled with the Holy Spirit and live a holy life;
  - teaching believers and strengthening their faith.

...to help others who feel God's call to ministry.

...to continue to study and to learn.

...to maintain his or her spiritual life through personal devotions.

The administrative duties of the pastor are...

...to receive people into membership.

...to oversee the various departments of the church (NYI, NMI, Sunday school and discipleship, women's fellowship, men's ministry, etc.).

...to prepare a report to the annual church meeting and to give a report to the district assembly.

...to make sure all money that is collected is spent properly.

...to sign official documents, sometimes with the secretary of the church.

The call and installation of the pastor

When a church wants to invite someone to become its pastor, it must follow the following steps [¶115-119]. This is what we mean by the phrase "calling a pastor."

1. **The church board meets with the district superintendent.** The superintendent will help the church board to find the right person. The board must choose an elder or a person with a minister's license to be the pastor. At least two-thirds of the members of the board must agree on the person, and the district superintendent must approve the decision. The person is then known as the candidate.

2. **The church board presents the candidate's name to the congregation.** The members of the church will vote "yes" or "no" on whether or not they want to invite

the candidate to become their pastor. At least two-thirds of the votes must be "yes" in order to elect the candidate.

3. **The church board and the candidate make arrangements.** The church board and the candidate will clearly communicate their goals and expectations to each other in writing. This includes the salary that the new pastor will receive.

4. **The candidate responds.** The candidate must reply to the call within 15 days. After accepting, he or she becomes the pastor.

5. **The installation service.** If possible, the district superintendent will organize an installation service where the new pastor and the congregation will celebrate their unity and direction. If the superintendent cannot be present, the church and pastor may organize the service by themselves.

In some cases, the church board does not vote on a new pastor. Instead, the district superintendent and the advisory board appoint a pastor. This happens in the following cases.

- The church is not yet five years old.
- The church has less than 35 members.
- The church receives regular financial assistance from the district.

The resignation of a pastor

A pastor may resign from a church by writing a letter to the church board and sending a copy to the district superintendent. If the church board accepts the resignation and the district superintendent approves it in writing, then the resignation becomes official. However, the pastor must continue to serve the church for 30 days after the resignation is accepted.

The pastor will work with the church secretary to prepare a correct list of all the names and addresses of the church members, which is called the membership roll. This list must have the same number of names as recorded in the most current district journal, with deletions and additions for the current year [¶120-121].

The relationship between the pastor and the church

Every two years the pastor and the church board have a meeting to review the expectations, goals, and performance of the church and pastor. We call the agreement "the Local Church/Pastoral Relationship" [¶122].

The district superintendent must be told of the meeting so that he or she may participate. The aim of the meeting is to take care of any problems and differences and to find solutions in an atmosphere of love, acceptance, and forgiveness. If a member of the board is the spouse of the pastor, he or she will not be part of the review process [¶123.1].

After a pastor completes two years of service as pastor, the church board, the pastor, and the district superintendent will meet. Like normal, they will discuss the relationship between the pastor and the church. However, at this meeting the district superintendent (or a representative) will work with the board to see if it wants to ask the pastor to continue for four more years [¶123].

The church board

Every church has a board. The members of the church board are as follows.

- The pastor
- The stewards
- The trustees
- The superintendent of the Sunday School and discipleship
- The NYI president
- The NMI president

In some cases, additional people will be elected to the church board, but it will not have more than 25 members. If there are ministers (ordained or licensed) who are members of the congregation but do not have a ministerial assignment, they are not eligible to be on the church board.

Church board members must represent the very best of what it means to be a Nazarene. The church should elect those who believe in entire sanctification, who live godly lives, and who support the church and its doctrines. They should also be faithful in attendance and tithing.

The church board meets at least once every two months. Some church boards meet every month [¶127-128].

The duties of the church board are...

...to work with the pastor to look after the church.

...to call a new pastor.

...to work with the pastor to develop a written statement of their goals and expectations. This is done every year, and it includes the pastor's salary.

...to arrange for someone to preach if there is no pastor.

...to review the relationship between the church and the pastor every two years.

...to elect a treasurer and secretary. The pastor is the chairperson of the church board.

...to elect at least three people to form an evangelism and church membership committee.

...to make sure that the financial obligations of the church are paid. This includes the Nazarene "budgets" (funds for the operations of the district, schools, and the World Evangelism Fund).

...to make sure that all church finances are supervised properly. A finance report is required

for every church board meeting and for the annual church meeting.

...to appoint at least two people to count all church offerings.

...to prepare a budget to cover the work of the church each year. This budget must also include amounts for NMI, NYI, Sunday School, schools and other organizations of the church.

...to assign people to a committee to monitor the finances and to report to the board if there are any problems.

...to approve or renew the license of local preachers or lay pastors, if the pastor recommends them. If a local preacher has a license for at least one year, the church board may recommend to the district assembly that he or she receive a minister's license.

...to arrange a sabbatical for the pastor every seven years.

The church board has a lot of responsibility. In addition to all of the duties listed, the church board is also responsible for all other affairs that are not specifically assigned to the pastor [¶129-130].

The church secretary

The church board elects the secretary, who must be a member of the church.

The duties of the church secretary are...

...to write the minutes of all church meeting and all church board meetings. "Minutes" are official records of all the activity of a meeting. The secretary should make sure that they are carefully preserved. The minutes should always include the names of all the board members and whether they were present or absent.

...to give a report to the church meeting of the activities of the church including the number of church members.

...to look care for all the legal papers belonging to the church.

...to tell the district superintendent the results of a vote for a pastor.

...to sign, with the pastor, the legal documents of the church.

[¶135]

The church treasurer

The church board elects the treasurer, who must be a member of the church.

The duties of the church treasurer are...

...to receive the offerings on behalf of the church and to spend the church's money when authorized to do so by the church board.

...to record all income and expenditure in a proper financial record book.

...to give a report to the church meeting and every church board meeting.

[¶136]

The stewards

The role of the steward in the church is to help in areas of practical service to others. All stewards are also members of the church board. They are elected at the annual church meeting, or the church board may assign some board members to be stewards. The stewardship committee encourages people to give generously of time, talent, and money to the Lord's work.

The stewardship committee consists of at least three but not more than 13 members.

The duties of the stewards are...

...to oversee the various outreach efforts of the church, including evangelism and starting new churches.

...to provide help to people who are needy and troubled. They should encourage, visit, and care for the sick and needy. Also, they should involve other church members in ministry to needy people in the community.

...to help the pastor, as needed, to prepare and to serve communion.

...to serve as the evangelism and church membership committee and church growth *committee if the church does not vote separately for these committees.*

[¶137-140]

The trustees

The role of the trustee is to be responsible for the church building and property. Like stewards, all trustees are also members of the board. During the annual church meeting, the members of the church will elect trustees to the church board, or the church board may assign some of its members to be trustees. There will be at least three but not more than nine trustees.

The duties of the trustees are...

...to oversee the use and maintenance of all the land and buildings belonging to the church.

...to help develop the financial plans for the church, including the pastor's salary.

[¶141-144]

The education committee (Sunday School)

The education committee is responsible for looking after the work of the Sunday School, discipleship, children's club, Bible studies, and all of the teaching ministries of the church. Officially, the name of this committee is the Sunday School and Discipleship Ministries International Board. Often we call it, simply, the SDMI board or the Sunday School board. In churches with less than

75 members, the church board may act as the education committee.

The members of this committee are...

...the president of the education board (SDMI). This person is often called the Sunday School superintendent.

...the pastor

...the president of the missions committee (NMI)

...the president of the youth council (NYI)

...the president of the children's committee

...the president of any adult ministries

...at least three but no more than nine members elected to the committee at the annual church meeting.

The task of this committee is to reach the largest number of unchurched people possible for Christ.

The goals of the SDMI are...

...to find ways to bring people into the church fellowship.

...to teach the Word of God effectively.

...to teach the doctrines of the Christian faith.

...to help the people of the church become Christlike disciples in character, attitudes, and habits.

...to help strengthen Christian homes.

...to prepare believers for membership in the church.

...to equip the church members for appropriate Christian ministries.

...to choose the curriculum to be used in all of the church's educations programs.

...to nominate people to chair various committees. (The pastor will then approve the names and present them to the annual church meeting for election.)

[¶145-149]

The youth committee
(Nazarene Youth International)

The church's ministry to young people is organised by the NYI council. NYI stands for Nazarene Youth International. The NYI council's goal is to help to disciple young people.

The members of this committee are elected at an annual meeting of all youth and those who work with young people in the church. Only a member of the church may be elected to serve on the NYI council. The council is usually composed of a president, vice president, secretary, and treasurer. Additional members may be elected if necessary.

The goals of the NYI are...

...to help young people to accept Jesus Christ as their Saviour.

...to instruct them in the word of God and the doctrines of the church.

...to disciple them so that they grow in the Christian faith and holy character.

...to help them to become members of the church and active in the work of the church.

...to equip them so that they will be involved in ministry.

[¶150; 810]

The missions committee
(Nazarene Missions International)

Most Nazarene churches organize an NMI council to help focus on world evangelism and missionary work. NMI stands for Nazarene Missions International. The NMI council works in the local church to generate prayerful interest and support for the missionary work of the church in other countries. The NMI council is usually composed of a president, vice president, secretary, and treasurer. Additional members may be elected if necessary.

The goals of the NMI are...

...to encourage people to pray for those who are not yet Christians.

...to inform the church about the work of the church in other countries.

...to help young people to hear God's call and to give themselves to Christian service.

...*to encourage people to give generously to the work of world evangelism.*

[¶152-154.3; 811]

Other ministries of the church

Local churches will often organize additional groups and committees. For instance, many churches now have a women's fellowship and a men's ministry. These are not all listed in the Manual, but they should be organized in a similar way to the NMI and the NYI. It is a good idea if the presidents of these groups also serve on the church board just like the NYI president and NMI president.

CHAPTER SIX

THE DISTRICT

The local Nazarene churches in a geographical area are combined together to form a district. The leader of each district is called the district superintendent. Each year representatives from all the local churches meet together in what is called a district assembly. Each district is part of a larger group of districts called a region, led by a regional director. Some regions also group districts together into fields, which are led by a field strategy coordinator

There are three different levels of districts [¶200.2].

Phase 1

When the Church of the Nazarene begins to work in a new country or a new area, it is called a phase 1 district. The regional director recommends someone to be appointed as the superintendent. The general superintendent will make the final decision and appoint the person to the post.

Phase 2

A phase 2 district has at least 10 organized churches, 500 full members and 5 ordained elders.

At least half of the finances needed for district administration will come from within the district.

The advisory board of a district may request that it be recognized as a phase 2 district. If the regional leadership believes that a phase 1 district is ready to move to the next phase, they will make a recommendation to the Board of General Superintendents who will make the decision. The district superintendent may be elected or appointed.

Phase 3

A Phase 3 district is one that demonstrates mature leadership, financial support, faithfulness to the doctrines of the church, and a vision for the growth of the global church.

A phase 3 district has at least 20 organized churches, 1,000 members, 10 ordained elders, and raises all the money needed for district administration.

The district superintendent will be elected by the district assembly.

The district assembly

Each district holds a special meeting once a year called the district assembly. At this meeting, the representatives from the local churches elect district leaders, conduct business, and hear reports from pastors and district boards. It is also a time for worship, fellowship, and training for service in the church. It is an opportunity to build enthusiasm and emphasise the vision and mission of the district.

The general superintendent decides the date and time of the district assembly. The district superintendent and the district advisory board decide where the district assembly will be held [¶201- 204].

The members of the district assembly are...

...*all ordained ministers (elders and deacons)*

...*all pastors with minister's licenses issued by the district assembly*

...*the district secretary*

...*the district treasurer*

...*the district SDMI president*

...*the district NYI president*

...*the district NMI president*

...*the presidents of any other district councils*

...*the newly elected Sunday School superintendent of each local church*

...*the newly elected NYI presidents of each local church*

...*the newly elected NMI presidents of each local church*

...*the members of the district advisory board*

...*the delegates of each local church*

The local church's delegation to the district assembly

The delegates of the local church are usually elected at their church's annual meeting. Sometimes, the church decides to allow the church board to select its delegates. All delegates must be lay members of their local church. A layperson is someone who is not an ordained minister and does not have a minister's license from the district.

The number of delegates from each church depends on two things: the number of members of a local church and the number of members of the district [¶201.1-201.2].

A church that is part of a district with fewer than 5,000 members, may elect two delegates if it has 50 or fewer members. It may elect one extra delegate for each additional group of fifty members. For instance:

50 church members : 2 delegates

51 to 100 members : 3 delegates

101 to 150 members : 4 delegates

151 to 200 members : 5 delegates

For larger districts that have 5,000 or more members, each local church sends one fewer delegate. So:

50 church members : 1 delegate

51 to 100 members : 2 delegates

101 to 150 members : 3 delegates

151 to 200 members : 4 delegates

This means that each local church may send the following people to the district assembly.

- The pastor (if he or she is licensed or ordained)
- The Sunday School superintendent
- The NYI president
- The NMI president
- At least one delegate, and more depending upon the size of the church.

The work of the district assembly

The duties of the district assembly are to receive reports, to elect leaders, and to transact other business. The district assembly will also elect members to various positions as leaders and members of committees. Some of these positions are for more than one year, so not all of these will be elected every time the district assembly meets together. The district assembly will also perform other official actions, based on recommendations that come from its committees and local churches.

The district assembly will receive reports from...

...the district superintendent [¶205.2]

...each ordained minister and anyone who has a minister's license issued by the district [¶205.3]

...the advisory board [¶222.25]

The district assembly will elect...

...the district superintendent

...*the advisory board*

...*the board of ministry*

...*the Sunday School board of the district*

...*the delegates to the General Assembly (once every four years)*

...*other boards and committees*

Every year is different, but generally the district assembly will also...

...*grant minister's licenses to pastors who are not yet ordained*

...*approve pastors for ordination*

...*approve pastors from other denominations to become pastors in the Church of the Nazarene*

...*review and approve the reports of the district*

The district superintendent

The district superintendent is the leader of the district and must be an ordained elder in the Church of the Nazarene. In Phase 1 districts, the district superintendent is appointed by the general superintendent. In Phase 2 districts, the district superintendent may be appointed or elected. In Phase 3 districts, the district superintendent is elected by the district assembly. In order to be elected, a person must receive votes from two-thirds of the district assembly members [¶209.1].

After completing two years, the district superintendent may be re-elected. A district superintendent may be re-elected without anyone else on the ballot. In this case, the district assembly members will vote "yes" or "no." The district superintendent must receive positive votes from two-thirds of the members to be re-elected. If re-elected, he or she will serve for four years [¶208].

If a district superintendent resigns or is not re-elected, the district assembly will continue to vote until someone is elected. The delegates may vote for any elder in the Church of the Nazarene. They will keep voting until one elder receives two-thirds of the votes.

The work of the district superintendent

The district superintendent may be a pastor of a local church. However, he or she has a lot of work to do [¶211–218.1].

The district superintendent helps local churches and leads the district.

Helping local churches

The district superintendent is sometimes called "the pastor to the pastors." He or she also works with local churches in many other ways. The duties of the district superintendent are...

...to organize, strengthen, and encourage local churches.

...to meet with church boards to review the work of the pastor.

...to help church boards call a new pastor.

...to meet with church boards and pastors that
  need help in times of trouble (spiritual, financial,
  pastoral, etc.).

...to help guide mission churches, stations, and
  preaching points that are not yet organized.

...to approve someone for a local preacher's license,
  if the pastor is not ordained.

...to conduct the annual church meeting of a local
  church if there is no pastor or if there is trouble in
  the church.

...to approve requests from pastors and church
  boards to employ someone as a paid minister,
  such as a youth minister or an associate pastor.

Leading the district

Working with the advisory board, the district
superintendent is responsible...

...to present a clear vision for evangelism, church
  planting, church growth, and the development of
  churches on the district.

...to chair the advisory board.

...to conduct the district assembly if the general
  superintendent is not present.

...to be a member of all district boards and
  committees.

...to appoint a replacement if a district leader
  resigns from a position, for example the district
  secretary or the district treasurer.

The district superintendent shall not spend district money without the approval of the advisory board. Her or she and all immediate family members (spouse, parents, children, and siblings) shall not be allowed to sign checks on any district account without the approval of the district assembly and the written authorisation of the advisory board [¶217].

The district secretary

The district secretary is elected by the advisory board. He or she serves for one, two, or three years and may be re-elected [¶219-221].

The duties of the district secretary are...

...to record correctly the actions of the district assembly and to preserve the minutes and statistics.

...to send a copy of all district reports to the field office.

...to refer any requests or items of business to the proper committee.

...to look after all the legal papers that belong to the district.

The district treasurer

The district treasurer is elected by the advisory board. He or she serves for one, two, or three years and may be re-elected [¶222–223.2].

The duties of the district treasurer are...

...to receive and disburse the district's money. The treasurer must follow the policies and directions of the advisory board and the district assembly.

...to keep a careful record of all money received and spent, and to prepare financial reports. The treasurer will give a monthly report to the district superintendent.

...to give an annual report to the district assembly.

The advisory board

The members of this board are elected each year at the district assembly. Pastors who have a minister's licence may not serve on the advisory board. The board helps the district superintendent lead and govern the district [¶224-228].

The members of this board are...

...the district superintendent

...up to three ordained ministers

...up to three laypersons

If a district grows beyond 5,000 members, it is allowed to elect additional members to the advisory board.

The district superintendent chairs the advisory board. In phase 1 and phase 2 districts, the field strategy coordinator may appoint a missionary representative to serve on it.

The duties of this board are...

...to counsel the district superintendent concerning the ministers and local churches on the district. They also give advice related to any district board or committee.

...to elect a district treasurer and a district secretary.

...to give a recommendation to the district assembly for anyone who is applying for a district minister's license or pastors who want to renew their license.

...to oversee all the property and buildings belonging to the district.

...to examine the testimony, background, and ordination papers of a pastor from another denomination who desires to join with the Church of the Nazarene.

...to handle the transfer of ministers to other districts and those coming from other districts.

...to perform other official duties that are not explicitly assigned to the district superintendent.

The board of ministry

This board is responsible for evaluating and developing those who are in the process of becoming ordained ministers. Sometimes this board is broken into two boards: the ministerial credentials board and the ministerial studies board. [¶205.17]

The ministerial credentials board

This committee has at least five elders. The district superintendent is a member and chairs the meetings. The board will elect a secretary to keep a good record of all the decisions of the board. The members carefully examine anyone who desires to receive a minister's license or to be ordained. If a pastor has a minister's license, then he or she must be approved by this board every year until he or she is ordained.

The board evaluates the person in three areas [¶229-231.10].

1. Christian experience. Someone who wants to become a minister in the Church of the Nazarene must have a clear experience of salvation and of being filled with the Holy Spirit. The board will look for evidence that the person has gifts and graces for ministry.

2. Beliefs. The board will ask questions to ensure that the person has a good knowledge of the Bible as well as the doctrines of the Church of the Nazarene. They will also ask questions to make sure that he or she accepts those doctrines as true, and not just as something to be studied.

3. Lifestyle. Anyone who wants to be a minister in the Church of the Nazarene must support the standards of conduct and follow the church's rules.

The ministerial studies board

This committee has five or more elders. It watches over the study programme of those people who are working toward ordination. The members encourage, guide, and assist them in their training [¶232-234.4].

The district Sunday School board (SDMI)

The official name of this group is the District Sunday School and Discipleship Ministries International Board. Most of the time, though, people call it the Sunday School board or the SDMI board. It supervises all the district activities for Christian education.

The board elects a secretary, a treasurer, and the directors of three district ministries: adults, children, and continuing lay education. These people become members of the SDMI board if they are not already on it [¶241-242.3].

The members of this board are...

...the district superintendent

...the district missions president (NMI)

...the district youth president (NYI)

...the chairperson of the board

...at least three elected members

The district youth council (NYI)

The official name of this group is the District Nazarene Youth International Council. Most people just call it the NYI council. It is responsible for planning ministry activities for young people on the district. The members of the council are elected at an NYI convention each year. There is a president, vice president, secretary and treasurer plus additional members and ministry directors [¶243].

The district missions council (NMI)

The official name of this group is the District Nazarene Mission International Council. Most people just call it the NMI council. It works to inform and inspire people about the evangelism efforts of the Church of the Nazarene around the world. The members of the council are elected at an NMI convention each year. There is a president, vice president, secretary, and treasurer plus three additional members [¶244].

Other boards and committees of the district

The district assembly may have other important committees and boards that help it function properly, including finance, organization of meetings, evangelism efforts, and many other tasks. The district superintendent is always a member of these boards, and they usually have an equal number of ministers and laypeople.

CHAPTER SEVEN

THE GENERAL ASSEMBLY

The Church of the Nazarene works in over 160 different countries. Every four years, delegates from those countries gather together in June for the its most important meeting: the General Assembly [¶301]. At this meeting, the delegates have authority to formulate doctrine and to make laws governing the church worldwide. The general superintendents chair the General Assembly.

The members of the General Assembly are...

...the delegates from all the districts around the world

...the general superintendents, including retired ones

...the directors and presidents of all the departments and ministries of the international Church of the Nazarene

Most of the members are delegates elected by districts. For phase 3 districts, half the delegates are laypersons and half are ordained ministers who have an assignment on the district. The district superintendent is one of the ministers. The rest are elected by the district assemblies. They will also elect alternates to replace a delegate who is unable to attend the General Assembly. The number of delegates from phase 3 districts depends on the number of members [¶301.1].

up to 6,000 members : four delegates
6,001 to 10,000 members : six delegates
10,001 to 15,000 members : eight delegates
15,001 to 20,000 members : ten delegates
etc.

Phase 2 districts are allowed just two delegates. The ministerial delegate is the district superintendent, and the district assembly elects the lay delegate. Phase 1 districts may send the district superintendent as a delegate, but he or she cannot vote.

The work of the General Assembly

The General Assembly has a lot of work to do each time it meets [¶305-305.9].

The duties of the General Assembly are...

...to elect six general superintendents.

...to elect the members of the General Board, and other international boards and committees.

...to accept or reject resolutions to add, change, or delete parts of the Manual or the constitution of the Church of the Nazarene.

Districts may submit resolutions to be considered at General Assembly. These resolutions will first be sent to committees for discussion. These committees will then make recommendations to accept or to reject the resolution. All of the recommendations will eventually be sent to the General Assembly, which will discuss each one further and vote on it. This is the way in which the Manual of the church can be modified.

The Board of General Superintendents

There are six general superintendents who are all ordained elders. They must be between 35 and 68 years old when they are elected. The general superintendents supervise the work of the Church of the Nazarene around the world. The six general superintendents meet together every three months. Together, they are called the Board of General Superintendents. Each region is assigned a general superintendent who helps the districts in many ways [¶306-307.16; 315-324].

The general superintendents provide spiritual leadership of the church by...

...articulating the mission of the church

...casting vision for the future of the church

...ordaining ministers

...raising awareness of our theology

...providing general oversight of the work of the church

They provide administrative leadership of the church by...

...presiding over the General Assembly and the meetings of the General Board.

...presiding over each district assembly or appointing someone to take their place.

...presiding over ordination ceremonies. They ordain those ministers whom the district assembly elects to become elders or deacons. Sometimes, they will appoint someone else to conduct the ordination service.

...appointing district superintendents if there is a vacancy between district assemblies. They do this after consultation with the advisory board and the other leaders of the district.

...overseeing all the boards and departments of the general church.

...deciding, together with the General Board, how the World Evangelism Fund should be spent. This fund is commonly known as WEF, and it is the combined money donated by all churches from around the world to support the work of the denomination.

...interpreting the law and doctrines of the Church of the Nazarene.

...doing anything else they feel necessary to help the work of the church provided it is in harmony with the Manual of the Church of the Nazarene.

The General Board

There are about 40 members of the General Board, and they meet once each year. Each region may nominate lay members and ordained ministers to it. The number of members depends on the total number of Nazarenes on each region. They are then elected by the delegates to the General Assembly from that region. The general treasurer and the general secretary are also members. Additional members are elected by some of the international organizations of the Church of the Nazarene such as NYI and NMI.

The General Board cares for the total work of the church worldwide. It helps each department to work in harmony with the other departments. Together with the Board of General Superintendents, the General Board decides how to spend the World Evangelism Fund. The General Board hears reports from all the departments of the church [¶331-341].

The General Secretary

The general secretary is elected by the General Board. He or she keeps all the official records for the Church of the Nazarene, including the minutes of the General Assembly. The general secretary also keeps careful statistics of church membership, and preserves the legal documents and important papers of the Church [¶325].

The General Treasurer

The general treasurer is elected by the General Board. He or she looks after all the money received and spent by the international church [¶329].

CHAPTER EIGHT

THE NAZARENE MINISTER

The Church of the Nazarene insists that all believers should minister to their family, friends, and neighbours. However, it also recognizes that the Lord calls some men and women to the more official work of public ministry. When the church discovers someone who is called to this type of ministry, it is responsible to investigate that call and to give opportunities for the person to enter the ministry. In most cases, we call these people pastors though they might also be deacons.

In the Church of the Nazarene, we use the word "minister" to include both elders and deacons. When we use the word "clergy," we are talking about all ordained elders, ordained deacons, and those hold a district minister's license.

There are three levels of ministers in the Church of the Nazarene. They are:

1. **The local minister,** approved by the local church board [¶531]
2. **The licensed minister,** approved by the district assembly [¶532]
3. **The ordained minister,** approved by the district assembly and ordained by the general superintendent as an elder or a deacon. Or-

dination is a special ceremony where a minister is consecrated to the task of ministry.

The local minister

The local minister must be a member of the Church of the Nazarene. He or she is licensed by the local church board and works under the pastor's direction. This gives local ministers the opportunity to use and develop their ministerial gifts. When a person receives a local minister's license, he or she enters into a process of lifelong learning.

If the pastor of the local church is an elder, then the local church board may issue the license, which is signed by the church secretary and pastor. If the pastor of the local church is not an elder, then his or her recommendation must be approved by the district superintendent.

Before a person receives a local license, the pastor and board must examine his or her experience of salvation, understanding of the doctrines of the Bible, and knowledge of the Manual. Candidates must demonstrate that they have the necessary spiritual gifts for ministry and are spiritually mature.

The license is for one year, but it may be renewed. The local minister must pursue the course of study for ministers. If, after two years, the minister has not completed two courses, the license will not be renewed.

A local minister does not officiate at marriages, nor does he or she administer the sacraments of baptism and the Lord's Supper. He or she is still considered to be a layperson.

The licensed minister

The next level of ministry comes with recognition from the district assembly. Applicants must be members of the Church of the Nazarene and must have a clear call to lifetime ministry. Here are the requirements for a local minister to receive a minister's license from the district:

- The applicant must be a local minister who has held a local minister's license for at least one year.
- The applicant must receive the approval of his or her local church board. If he or she is the pastor of a church, the advisory board must approve.
- The applicant must have completed one full year of an approved course of study, usually through a Bible college (or the equivalent), and must promise to continue to pursue the course of study for ministers.
- The applicant must carefully fill out an application for a minister's license and submit it to the board of ministry.
- The applicant will be interviewed by the board of ministry to determine whether or not he or she is fit for the work.

- The applicant must receive a favourable vote by the district assembly.

The licensed minister is either working toward becoming an elder or a deacon. Once a person receives the initial license, he or she has ten years to complete the course of study for ministers.

Those who have a minister's license from the district may be assigned as pastors of churches on their district. As long as they pass the required courses of study, they have the authority to preach and administer the sacraments to their own congregations. If local laws allow it, the licensed minister may also officiate marriages.

Licensed ministers from other evangelical denominations may request a transfer to serve in the Church of the Nazarene. They must present their credentials to the advisory board. If they pursued a course of study equivalent to that of the Church of the Nazarene, and if they meet all the other requirements listed above, the district assembly may grant a minister's license.

The district license is for one year, but it may be renewed. Once a license is given, the pastor must meet the following requirements in order to have the license renewed.

- The minister must hold a district license and complete an application for renewal each year.
- The minister must be approved by the advisory board.

- The minister must have completed at least two more courses in the course of study.
- The minister must demonstrate that he or she has spiritual gifts and usefulness for the work.
- The minister must be approved by the board of ministry and the district assembly.
- The minister cannot renew a license after ten years unless there are special circumstances.
- The minister must have the goal to be ordained as an elder or deacon in the Church of the Nazarene.

The ordained minister

In the Church of the Nazarene, we recognize two types of ordained ministers: the deacon and the elder.

The ordained deacon

The deacon is a person who feels called to full time Christian service, but not a call to preach. Some deacons serve as full time workers with children or youth, some work as hospital chaplains, some do full time visitation work in a large church, and others are involved full time in compassionate ministries.

The deacon is given authority to administer sacraments, and on occasion to conduct worship and preach. The steps to become an ordained deacon are the same as those to become an ordained elder except that there are some differences in the required studies [¶533].

The ordained elder

The position of ordained elder is for those who have a clear call from God to preach his Word. We expect our pastors to give their full energy to a lifetime of Christian service. This is a permanent position and the ordination does not need to be renewed every year [¶534].

A pastor with a minister's licence must complete many requirements in order to be ordained as an elder. He or she must ...

> ...*graduate from a validated course of study for ministers.*

> ...*serve as a pastor for three consecutive years (or more) while holding a district license. For ministers serving part-time, the district may require more than three years of service.*

> ...*receive the recommendation for renewal of the minister's license by the church board or the advisory board.*

> ...*be carefully evaluated and approved by the board of ministry and receive its recommendation.*

> ...*be in good standing with the church. This means that there are no disqualifications on his or her record.*

> ...*receive a favourable vote of two-thirds of the members of the district assembly to recommend the candidate for ordination.*

IS GOD CALLING YOU TO BE A MINISTER?

If you think that God might be calling you to be a pastor or deacon, it is important to seek the wise council of other believers, especially your pastor. While you may begin the process of studying for the ministry, only the pastor and church board are able to grant you a local minister's license, and only someone who has a local minister's license for at least one year may apply for a district license.

The ordination of a new elder or deacon happens at a special service conducted by the general superintendent, usually at the time of the district assembly. The general superintendent along with the other elders and deacons will lay hands on the minister and ordain him or her as an elder or deacon in the Church of the Nazarene.

Recognition of credentials from other denominations

Ordained ministers from other evangelical denominations who desire to unite with the Church of the Nazarene will be examined by the board of ministry as to their conduct, personal experience, and doctrinal beliefs [¶535]. If approved, they may transfer their credentials to the district. These are the steps:

- They must meet all the other requirements listed above.
- They must complete a course on the Manual of the Church of the Nazarene.
- They must complete a special form and send it to the district secretary.
- They must be currently serving in a ministry assignment.

The general superintendent will issue a certificate of recognition, signed by the district superintendent and the district secretary.

Retirement from the ministry

The office of ordained minister is permanent, which means that it does not have to be renewed each year. The minister is required to give an annual report to the district assembly. When an elder or deacon retires from the ministry, the district assembly will make a note in the district journal. The minister's name will remain on the list for the district, but he or she will not be required to make a report to the district assembly [¶536].

The resignation or removal from the ministry

The ordination certificate is like a contract between the minister and the denomination. It is only valid as long as the minister's life and teaching are in accordance with the doctrines and practices of the church.

Ordained ministers will not regularly conduct independent church activities that are not under the direction of the Church of the Nazarene without the approval of the advisory board. If an elder or a deacon joins another denomination, he or she ceases to be an elder or deacon of the Church of the Nazarene [¶539.4]. That is to say, his or her name will be removed from the district roll of ministers.

A minister may resign from the ministry by sending his or her credentials to the district superintendent who will send it to the general secretary for safekeeping [¶539]. A minister who remains unassigned for four or more years may be listed as "removed" by the district assembly [¶539.2].

Sadly, sometimes it is necessary to discipline a member of the clergy. If serious accusations are proven to be true, the elder or deacon's name will be removed from the roster of ministers. This may be caused by serious misconduct or teaching doctrines out of harmony with the articles of faith. More details about this process are found in the Manual [¶539; 606.1].

CONCLUSION

The Church of the Nazarene is a wonderful organization, but an organization is only as good as its people. Nazarenes are some of the finest people in the world.

The Manual of the Church of the Nazarene may seem like a boring book of rules, policies, and procedures. However, it exists to help our church become more effective in accomplishing its great task to "Go and make disciples of all the nations." It exists to help those disciples become more and more like Christ. It exists so the Kingdom of God will expand and grow and that many new people will discover what it means to live in holiness and love God with their whole hearts.

So as we work together, pastors and lay people, let us remember these words from the Bible.

GOD'S WORD TO CHURCH MEMBERS

"You are God's dear children, so try to be like him. Live a life of love. Love others as Christ loved us" (Ephesians 5:1, ERV).

GOD'S WORD TO PASTORS AND CHURCH LEADERS

"Keep watch over yourselves and all the flock of which the Holy Spirit has made you overseers. Be shepherds of the church of God, which he bought with his own blood" (Acts 20:28).

"Be shepherds of God's flock that is under your care, serving as overseers not because you must, but because you are willing, as God wants you to be; not greedy for money, but eager to serve; not lording it over those entrusted to you but being examples to the flock. And when the Chief Shepherd appears, you will receive the crown of glory that will never fade away" (1 Peter 5:3-4).

9781563448355